# *Waiting for the Paraclete*

# WAITING FOR THE

LISE GOETT

# *Paraclete*

Introduction by Carol Frost

BARNARD NEW WOMEN POETS SERIES

Beacon Press
Boston

BEACON PRESS
25 Beacon Street
Boston, Massachusetts 02108–2892
www.beacon.org

Beacon Press books are published under the auspices of
the Unitarian Universalist Association of Congregations.

06  05  04  03  02    8  7  6  5  4  3  2  1

This book is printed on acid-free paper that meets the uncoated
paper ANSI / NISO specifications for permanence as revised in 1992.

Text design by Christopher Kuntze
Composition by Wilsted & Taylor Publishing Services

Library of Congress Cataloging-in-Publication Data

Goett, Lise.
  Waiting for the Paraclete / Lise Goett ; introduction by Carol Frost.
    p. cm.—(Barnard new women poets series)
ISBN 0–8070–6867–5 (acid-free paper)
I. Title. II. Series.
PS3607.O34 W35 2002
811'.6—dc21                                    2001006371

FOR MY PARENTS

*We have dreamt the world. We have dreamt
it as firm, mysterious, visible, ubiquitous in space
and durable in time; but in its architecture we
have allowed tenuous and eternal crevices
which tell us it is false.*

JORGE LUIS BORGES

*Save all of yourself for the wedding though
nobody knows when or if it will come.*

CARLOS DRUMMOND DE ANDRADE

# Contents

IV

# Introduction

Carol Frost

Is poetry untranslatable or does it, as in Borges' statement about the world, carry enough that is "tenuous and eternal" in its architecture to allow, despite all the earth's firmness and visibility, that our sense of things may be false or incomplete? In other words, isn't poetry something we recognize aside from the multiplicities of style and language, native or otherwise, and line? Lise Goett's strengths, for instance, lie in the truth-telling that knows it contains lies, and in flirtations with beauty; hers is a poetry one doesn't easily get over. Lines as abstract as "into the omega / of not-being" and as plain as "on a tricycle" lean against, and into, a vision of "the very existence of things"—things commonplace and strangely lifted into rapture. When she writes, "I am fascinated by something / scorched, / something passed over and awaiting / the final election by fire" (in "Where Earth, This Fire"), she gives us in clear and simply beautiful language the secret of what poetry must do to effect the "astonished release" of body and the tangible into smoke, soul, or spirit—the unfinished realm where poetry goes if it is to last. For the real to burnish into the poetic, something else must remain behind, for reality and poetry are impure. Poetry leaves its traces—"bee-thrum," "Telstar," "a horse named Riverland Sally," "dinner coffee," "the earth's inner clocks," "white wicker chairs," "the Ohio River," "charming Death," and "love's incalculable averages."

Where the single phrases and paragraphs of original beauty lie, a common reader looks for something else—less, I think, for Coleridgian "balance and reconciliation," where freshness and the familiar, passion and order (all opposing parts and possibilities in art) are rendered whole, than for what may be called a failed alchemy. The reader looks for residue rather than gold. To make the venerable thing, something more is always needed, and the reader looks for a sense that the poet may know at last what it is. The chunk of gold is unattainable, but the ingredients in the glass pear bubble and smoke. It is in Goett's "ghostly equivalents" and the "burning" in the gut where poetry is revealed—abstractly, materially, really, falsely. Poetry can be translated. Poetry isn't whole.

I

## Something Close

It is hard to begin with a death,
albeit metaphorical,
of what you thought would be your future.
You look out as the rain pelts the neighborhood mansards
and think you could tell
she was calling him to come to the phone
while she was reading a book in the kitchen.

They are not newly in love.
You gauge the distance between bodies as confidence
and remember how, amid the cold litmus of ether and air
    where you lived,
he could hardly bear your parting—
as if the very existence of things might then vanish,
as if underneath everything hummed a desire.
You said, *You are the palmer; and I am the strict, white margin*
    *of the body.*
And he said, *Life goes on. It is normal.*

In the street below,
a child spools out from his mother,
then returns to the discipline of the margin
like verse.
It is not
that you were not
as it seemed
a January of tulips flushed in their waxy abundance;
it is not that what broke was not crystal
but that buried with or wedded to the intensity of things
is this notion of parting.

The rain comes less hard now, lightening in intervals,
and you think of the river where they live,
how the rain must be pocking it now, its halcyon currents,
rain starring the hills of narcissus, the houses rumpled in
     smoke.
You wanted him to remember you like that, as viaticum
for the divine body, the last journey,
so stunned were you in disbelief of love's incalculable averages.

The sojourners have gone,
the arm-in-arm strollers
taking their light,
and you lean toward that river,
as if making provision
to hear some more acute music
from the other side.

## After Twenty Years of Marriage

I saw it in a book on diseases of the mouth,
the smile that is heaven, the smile I cannot reach:
the youth known only by some gesture in the street
but held and loved in memory like honeyed plums
dripping through the slats back home—
the way the body does not want to separate from coitus
even though the love has died and failed us.
And so taking for a season these summer rooms,
we couched ourselves in the satin sheen of marble walks,
the tristesse of linen trousers, of peacocks
garnishing the lawns, while our friend,
to make us see and feel the world stripped of its skin,
described the paddocks where he sodomized his father's
      grooms
among the smell of Thoroughbreds and leather.
We drank and lay like corpses in our summer suits
and rationed love like gasoline in wartime.
And after dinner coffee, and after coffee chocolates,
the soul rapt in a soulless argument
making the afternoon sway
like the slow turning of the world upon its axis
as we sat and watched the shadows lengthen
from our Adirondack chairs—
that marriage of bodily fluids, Europe, death
which sunset sometimes betokens.
The sun, descending upon its worried tether,
rendered up its climax; and the sky
seemed more poignant for being faint
(like attenuated cries from distant hotel rooms)
in the afterglow of dusk. So Goya said:
*Let us make love then* under the roiling stars

even as the acids fade this corroded city.
This star, long burnt out, in whose light we make our truce,
like some light coming from the dead,
touches—one might even say blesses—
our oceangoing scow as it makes its difficult passage,
violet bleeding into dusk.

# Antediluvian

### I

On the door, the butcher's quaint bell—like an altar boy's—
rings my arrival. *This is the introit,* it says, the butcher's apron
pink with intimations of blood.

He is my rose-pale Amundsen.
Three times a day, he enters the tomb.
Here are the frozen-in-death, the struck-in-mid-lowing:
immaculate doves of the Spirit,
fatted calves with eyes rolled to the backs of their heads,
six-pointed stags—
all stripped and hung from their grapplings.

The butcher asks me what I am cooking today.
This is part of our ritual.
His fingers raw from the slaughterhouse,
he hands me white packages, appendages sawed off,
with the heft or weight of a sacrament.
There is nothing we would not kill
with our appetites.

### II

From her glass catafalque, at the Chapel of the Miraculous
     Medal,
the patron saint of all spinsters
displays her flesh, undecomposed.
A sign says, *No Latin rite today.* A rosary is noosed
around her petrified hands.
Catherinettes make their way to the altar;
they cross themselves and pray for a man,

then pass through the great doors
where the living and their ghostly equivalents
ask for life in the vernacular: *spare change.*


### III

At night, you put your cold hands on my breasts,
take me up by the chine bone, swivel me around.
Hearts unhooked from their scaffolds,
we lower our heads to our need,
our teeth chipping away at what can no longer be said
until we've chewed down to the bone,
until we are no longer man and woman,
but glistening bodies of water, a lip—
the loins' pallor and flame mute as doves
under ice.

We'll go on like this until something happens,
until a river runs through the house
and washes everything away;
then in the morning we'll rise, we'll begin,
stick by stick as we always do,
to build our Babel again.

# Lingerie

> *Simplicity is the last thing learned.*
> CONFUCIUS

When first you came to Paris, you glided between
    subterranean poles,
a Eurydice tricked by a serpent into the underground,
but now you feel ready to leave it, sharing a glass of Sancerre
    with this man,
his voice charming Death, saying trust me,
I'll take you up through this darkness.
You think, What does this guy know about darkness,
his head of blond locks like wheat gleaned in summer light?
You are Eurydice knowing too well
that no one resurrects you save yourself.

And in this city where you have spent enough time
for each cell to be replaced in the body—waiting
according to the French way of thinking, weaning all but the
    fittest—
the attenuation of desire rendering arrival more exquisite,
you take solace in the logic behind lingerie:
the black bodice with its many hooks and closures,
the serpentine logic behind lacings as thin as vermicelli,
breasts riding the crests of Venusian half shells—
pigeonettes roosting serenely in their nests.

You are safe in your fortress, festooned in your elaborate armor,
tendering your many-layered love, teaching your lover
it takes time to enter the core.
He assiduously studies the primer: fastenings as complex as
    French legal code,

front closures designed for quick and ready release—pasta
with its bows and cups and shells—various shapes for holding
    the sauces.

And after all this journeying into difference,
the lyrist's turned look, five seconds separating you from
    union,
the confusion of mixed dates of departure and arrival
making of your heart this one thin target
that only the truest of marksmen can graze,
doesn't the soul come to rest in what it is?
The art of simple surrender is the last thing learned,
charm its own disarming armament. Arrayed
in all the seduction of your bright headdress,
you recognize the soil it comes from—
expert in the school of charming Death.

# Water-Hanger

You, too, have thought of women as creamy white callas,
unfurling themselves in the Greek town, exposing their white
    necks
when the temperature of evening is almost equal to the fluids
    of the body,
torsos in a rhapsody of movement along the Boule Mich
past the skewered meats of the Greek tavernas, trussed
    sucklings, *so much carnage,* you think,
a kind of pollination working its way up through the sorriest
    influences,
weaving a fecund grace as ripe as the rotund bellies of bees.

You, he, tourists in Nikes and T-shirts, a saxophonist
whose skin turns green under the neon light of some all-night
    den,
are the bees of this place, hoping to take some of this sweetness
    home,
the royal jelly of the human hive, the sweet Jesus rising out of
    the squalor
to which this music sings.

The fluencies of evening buoy you up, body you forth toward
    the quay
where you are meeting a friend in some decorator's idea of
    businessman chic—
gray banquettes, gray plates accented in peach—
reminding you of what a fortune-teller once told you:
Gray is the color of America's sexually blocked, and all you saw
    before you
were gray cars, gray suits, endless gray days adrift in secretarial
    pools.

So the next day you booked a flight for Paris, expecting to find
    satin sheets and baroque esplanades?

It has turned out to be a much longer journey than you
    thought:
a night cab ride over rain-slicked pavés, taking you within
    blocks of your desire,
then not, the driver veering into oncoming traffic
before halting at your destination where, by some freak of
    nature's symmetry,
you are a threesome, your film-director-cum-painter friend,
his sartorial wings outspanning you and your date like Jove in
    the Rider deck
as he waves away a dead fish in its unctuous pool of butter and
    asks,
*So where are you in your life?*

The sheer drop of your life astounds you as the human current
    carries you toward the Seine,
the white waters of your life riffling into its jet black waters:
owl blacks, blindfolded blacks, dark-night-of-the-soul blacks
flowing into the terror of white nights toward a precipice
where there is some question whether the water went over the
    cliff
but before it could call itself rapids, called itself back from full
    flowering
or is a cataract in the act of becoming.

Your heart, its one pale votive burning for the night when a
    thousand snowy egrets left in a cloud from a tree,
turns now toward the Notre-Dame de Paris, the serene face of
    the Madonna
buttressed for renovation like the sagging rites of this religion,
and receives the seeds of this evening, the honey trickling
    down into every life,

before you head toward the fields of the war god,
  remembering when
the lily of the angel insinuated itself into her darkness
with what fate or force engenders there.

# Convergence

When first you came to Paris,
you attended saturnalian balls
in chandeliered rooms with faux-marble walls,
French doors giving out onto jade copses.
Men, versed in the sports of the body,
fingered cigars in velour cases, eyed
you as gristle for their boiling oil,
the net of good fortune catching you in the nick.

You no longer grieve for the past;
but there are days, you admit,
when you yearn for the future.
Still, a burning persists in the gut,
all winter the doctor the only man you unveiled for,
your niggling diseases sentencing you
to some final apprenticeship
before the purest happiness comes.

Now your body resounds, taking the bus across town,
your body gliding slightly above it
as you survey the chestnut blossoms' tiered crowns,
a light haze coming into the treetops—
the reception of something so delicate
that if it isn't received it will die.
A frail insistence now emerges
into the effulgence of broad daylight.

Discarding the pallor of shrouds, of linen,
the earth's inner clocks releasing alchemical forces,
you will meet this fine day.

There will be oil enough to wait for the bridegroom.
There will be oil enough when the inner and outer align
to see your illumination in the face of the beloved,
all lanterns lit
like the raging garden of your father's old age—

delphiniums, nasturtiums—
the masterwork of the last stage, the last flowering,
born of a diligence so light-filled
that its equal is summoned again.

# II

## Conversion

All day, we loitered at the throat of the penny arcade
to hear how the fisherman's cast had taken the eye of Vilas
Puchomsky, a pain radiating down to the sexual curve.
Girls who had been prom queens, corsages of gallica roses
with crowning pink buds pinned to our blouses, teetered
on lives of uncloistered want to hear how the hook
had entered the pulp, tearing the flesh like a litchi nut
with the force of a swift and ready conversion.

At dusk, the fly-speckled marquee flickered with inconstant
    love;
and our boys suckled long-necked colas and pilsners,
and we asked them to hug us all the tighter while the nuns
    sang
from the hill, "Le Dieu Qui Nous Aime Bien," for it seemed
that the boy's name had called his fate into the world,
the line cutting through the air like the wing of a hawk,
his face buried in a shirt of bruised muslin.
And later, over the cracked and rutted road home, his story
came to us like a voice speaking from behind a steel grate,
a blue light hovering above the lake's teal horizon.

One day at school, he removed his eye and touched us,
tiered like the blessed and the damned in the bleachers
behind the parochial school, the glass eye sucking our arms
where lips might have gone, a touch like benediction—
a taste of terror with some pleasure in it, a pleasure
already sown with remorse and the seeds of turning away.

But at night, we prayed to a god with a foraging heart,
a god with a silvering face, rippling his luminous skin—

the line gilt along the line's trajectory, the plummet like shot—
thinking how grace must enter the body like this
as we slipped out under the nameless bowl of stars
to feel the hunger of our own darkness:
the sweep and whisper of the line,
the suck and gape of the eyeless socket,
the god who reels us in.

## Thanatos

The amphitheater holds them like a chalice:
fair-haired, blue-eyed boys
bused in from all four corners of the state
to hear the coroner's lecture on alcohol-related death.

His address could be the farm report:
his dry recital of quantities consumed,
absorption rates classed by weight,
his description of the slow, almost exquisite

paralysis of the brain followed by slides
of sundry decapitations. Then there it is, a corpse
spread-eagled across the screen, its eyes upraised like Christ's—
twinned cornflowers afloat in a milk-filled glass—

and everywhere a sea of the cheapest cans of beer,
not even the dying wish of a connoisseur in evidence.
But not a word is said about what makes a man
want to kill himself, that alpine lake that glimmers

in the reptile brain, or how he goes from room to room,
dousing the lights on each compartment of his life:
the kitchen with its garbage pail and rack of spoons;
the living room, its fold-out couch the marriage-bed

where he took his wife, a burning town inside her,
the sounds of small animals scaring out as she fit
over him like a silo. The sensible boys will go no further;
but there are a few, transfixed perhaps by the music of a voice

that stings them in the dark copses of their blood,
who would have followed Orpheus

to a lake as mysterious as the face of any stranger.
They want to touch its bottom, rub a bit of it

between their fingers. They step into the little heart-sac
of water that swells around them and feel *first chill*
*then stupor.* The evening lusters as they enter,
translucent as they leave themselves behind.

And in accordance with that psychoanalytic school,
they don't believe in death, or to put it in another way,
each one remains convinced of his own immortality
and, as on a dare, wants to see what survives the wreckage.

Their bodies ghost beneath the surface then disappear;
and then the good god Thanatos enters them
like grain force-fed through a funnel.
Their faces peaceful and sublime,

they feel nothing but the body's slight loosening;
and as they pass the point where others' lives have faltered,
they hear their mothers calling:
*You love life more than you know.*

# Blood Atonement

FOR GARY GILMORE

A ghost came to kiss
the boy in his bed.

Ghosts, his grandmother tells him,
never surrender. On her nightstand,

a Ouija's heart-shaped planchette spells out
*bad omen,* family histories written in charlatan ink.

A brick in a graveyard marks a plot
with no name: *Our Baby.*

The boy wears a cowboy shirt.
Behind him, a burning

smudges the sky with October.
Into the eye of a camera, he takes aim

at a spectator visible only to him,
his gun's deadly wick

razing his opponent
with two shots to the heart's chambers.

Years later, he shows the world his last trick of escaping,
a bull's-eye target pinned to his chest

as the five of his firing squad take aim,
the world calling down his erasure.

*There will always be a father,*
he says, the murdered pale as garments

the Mormons wear for the Rapture:
a clatter of bone,

all the dead rising together.
Night folds its black napkin,

each star a torn suture.
The boy's bones sing from a jar.

## American Gothic

Somewhere in Wisconsin, in one of those towns
that depends for its life on the river,
a couple gave birth to five children,
none of them "normal."

Perhaps you read in the paper what happened,
or heard it yourself in the Liquor and Health,
Southern Comfort and ginkgo biloba staring you down in the
    aisles.
*Another life taken by the river.*
You remember where you were when you heard it.
It's that kind of story:

*a current too strong for even a good swimmer to master.*
The newspaper shows the pontoons where they tried to call
the boy back, the point on the river where he was last seen
shining up like worn pewter.

In the bar, they're telling jokes about Bobby,
*slow Bobby, Bobby-who-died-in-the-river,*
but you're thinking about the time
you were headed toward Vernon,
thirty miles out of town on the highway,
and you saw a boy
tooling down the edge of the interstate
on a tricycle;
and by God, it was Bobby.

Some fat guy from Nebraska
wants to know the rest of the story.
The bartender wipes a glass, a gray scar at his wrist

slipping below his cuff as he gestures,
*All those retarded kids.*
*It's not as bad as you think.*
*It's a question of perspective,*
his voice cutting out like a plane's motor,

the world already described by a surfeit of words:
All Saints' Day, duck hunting over,
the slap of wet leaves like so many hands,
Frederickson's Cinderella display,
its carriage and six white horses holding out its dream
of survival.

And then only the river speaks:
*Who wouldn't want to be carried like this?*
*Who doesn't dream of surrender?*

## 1933

> *Dying's the best*
> *Of all the arts men learn in a dead place.*
> JAMES WRIGHT

Sometimes, on evenings like this, my mother will speak of
    Tom Scott,
going down to a place inside her beyond the river's high reach,
to a place where grief has no pallbearer except the river;
and I know she is thinking of that threadbare year of
    Depression, the year
my mother was released from the egregious care of the mother
superior, smiling for a portrait of the student body

in a coat purchased with the sale of a calf's stiffened body.
Or was it the color of her hair that pulled Tom Scott
toward her, the fox-collared coat being my grandmother's
idea of what a perfect lady of fashion should wear, past reach
of a farm-girl's dreams—or anyone's—that year
in Kentucky? As she walked on the banks of the Ohio, I think
    the river

must have been my mother's only true friend, the river-
slow current, its tracery, feeding my mother's love-starved body
as she waited for something to comfort her face; and her
    freshman-year
beau, a writer of talent, a man named Tom Scott,
cut rushes on prayerful diagonals along the river's high reach—
a bouquet for the girl who suggested that my mother

be kept apart from those who didn't work. My mother,
the poorest girl in her dormitory, waitressed at the river
café, working more shifts as she struggled to reach

the nickel she needed for graph paper, the twenty for Kotex,
    her body
a calendar, bleeding her, despite her good Scot
thrift, into greater and greater debt. The year

was 1933, what was to be their bridal year,
the year Tom Scott killed himself, cradling a mother-
of-pearl revolver, with two shots to the left ventricle, after
    Scott
lost his life savings on a horse named River-
land Sally in the Derby; and men said, Please God, no more
    bodies
in Lexington, Kentucky, where the stable boys still reach

to receive the reins of lost gentry as if reach-
ing could save them. In that damnable year,
who knows if she ever embraced Tom Scott's body
in the deep and silent green. My mother's
voice goes slack, the woof of her life shining up like a river
through that threadbare year and the death of Tom Scott.

And I wish I could reach into the past and hand my mother
that nickel for graph paper. Every year, the Ohio River
rises, claiming the body of another Tom Scott.

## Rescuers

And our conversation turns
to these stories
of our making and unmaking,
of what thing in the human heart makes us rescue.
And because I cannot bear to speak of the psychiatrists,
I say: They came,
each an illumined being,
with wings like human hands,
immune to fire's contagion or pain's.

Or perhaps the heart strips itself
and goes down,
shedding its various selves
to fathom the nature of drowning:
The honor of saving
is that the rescued kneels down
and puts his head
inside the jaws of the rescuer,
dying to all else except what the heart knows.

It is beginning to snow
as it does in the dreams of the unhearing,
and you keep on walking
past the city limits where night is loosed from its cages
(because your heart, hasn't it carried you this far?)
until you have extinguished all thought except the sweet face
    of the other,
the last bony finger of that mendicant spirit, your heart,
    tapping
until you can see God's ribs in the train tracks.

Later that spring, you'll return to those fires he built with his
    own clothing

to signal where help should come,
because the paraphernalia of saving
is something always waiting inside you,
making and unmaking,
as it did that night
among the rosy coils, the charred and still human fretwork.

## Numen

During one of those times
when I walked like a woman who doesn't care for herself,

like mist leaving a riverbed,
wherever I went the sparseness of angels,

I went out past the borders of town
and lay down with the silence of tractors.

Perhaps I wished to become a thing as senseless as straw,
to be tilled under then wake into springtime,

all around me grasses bending like wan girls
toward their sources. It was then

my mother told me about the boy who loved skylarks,
about his foot that ended in a paw,

about how he dragged all the dumb parts of his body
behind him to watch the birds in their glides

as they scissored,
plummeting at the end of their song

in the arcs of their ecstasy.
When your life is unskeined from its bolt,

the boy who loved skylarks sees
the wide wales of this whole and singular cloth.

He sees your body stripped of its bark,
your spatulate tongue,

your soul aglint like straw in the loam.
He sees all that is of the lark, and all that is not;

and he will parse you with the strictness of your sentences—
every pock, every stone.

# Where Earth, This Fire

*It is not that you do not see; it is that you are in
a painful stage of seeing.*
CAROLYN FORCHÉ

## I. PRELUDE

I am fascinated by something
scorched,
something passed over and awaiting
the final election by fire.

Slumped, alert, they lean forward,
for whom the burning change of the world
means nothing,
their preternatural faces staring
into the omega
of not-being.

God burned them, but not to death,
life being fear of death;
and when they lost the fear,
they became something we no longer recognized—
thoraxes flailing themselves alive against a porch light.

## II. ESCAPE

*Dried blood, gashed, smeared with the fingertips
torn out,
foxtails, pieces of sheared metal*

Smeared on the roadside,
the gorgeous, gorged youth,
burning bright and adamantine

under the cold quanta,
hurls himself
and in some prayer-like dervish
falls headlong,
splitting his body in astonished release.

And it is not
that the world did not see.
It is that the world did not recognize
the spirit
greater than the sum of its parts, lobotomized.


### III. Walking in the Ground

In the cool night air,
a woman, almost thirty,
goes out behind the woodpile,
tracking back like a retriever
to the first sweet molder of love.

Flailing in the moonlight,
it is as if something came alive there,
baptized and naked as snow—
the plumulae of desire awake in the dead body,
enticed up
through the body,
through its ten thousand astonishings
which are the recesses of memory.

And does not each of us go back,
trying to bury himself with the life of fermentation,
self-fooled into belief,
into the promised return of the loved one
by climbing into the ground,
remembering when

the man climbed into the womb of the woman
and in his astonished release
succeeded
in uniting—
he the fish swimming in and she the fish swimming out—
the womb of birth which is of water
and the womb of death which is of earth?


★


These are some theories
of transformation:
the first is to divest the spirit of the body
by suicide;
the second, self-resurrection
by masturbation;
the third takes the advice to the Jews:
go home
and wait,
close your doors,
this pain will pass over,

as each awaits the same deliverance,
the same approaching.

# III

# The After-Season

AFTER HENRY JAMES

Like child-anchorites sealed inside a wall,
we read our Book of Hours,

and make a Jolly Corner
of our Pisan villas in decline.

(In winter, how sad the lesions are,
the body's dappled rind, the breasts'

rich foison under eager hands.)
All perfume and simulacrum,

the evening is our habitat,
those empty Augusts when

light is music
and all Europe seems a vacancy.

We've lost the name of action,
but like some monstrous strain

of orchid which strikes the mind as tainted,
we have our reasons for withdrawal.

Our treasons make us beautiful,
as James would say: *in fine*. Viral birds-

of-paradise, we make our exits (silent, stunned),
we hangers-on of the after-season, holding on.

# Labyrinth

Look up. Your life is suddenly ending—
the pages yellow, the lamplight yellow—
the face of someone you love the halo
of autumn burning. The wending white string
which has taken you down so many corridors
is Ariadne's thread through the darkness.
Outside, the beast is shaking its harness.
Look up from the cracks in your
brown leather shoes into a room where someone
is working an acrostic that always spells *winter,*
snow falling thick on the serpentine walk, white wicker
chairs in a state of surrender. These are the lees
of the thoughts you can't master—the street
an archipelago numbed.

# Threnody

You cannot imagine the day of your death or how it might
    happen,
the day and the hour like islands bandaged in fog,
or how the flax of these hours will go spinning without you,
stitching and unstitching ineffable veils.

For the first time, the stigmataed shoots of the dogwood
strike you as alien; and the dragon scales of the hyacinth
yield a different new birth. When was it the years
seemed as broad as these doors giving out onto the quay

and prosperity outstretched like wide-cut lapels,
your father fondling uncut cigars at the Petroleum Club?
Now those tropics of burgeoning feeling, all having,
have given way to something as ghostly as actuarial charts,

neither subject nor object, those trains of expectancy never
    arriving—
and you a torn god on the quay with the lights turned out.
When you close your eyes, wearing your life like a garment,
you will no longer be here to see the world,

you will no longer be here to kiss these singular stones.
All passion tastes of relinquishment. The world is slipping
    away.
You who know music came before light have begun to hear
the arched crescendo of the dying song in each parched leaf

singing its threnody to the end of the world.
And even this music will continue without you,
those tiny white lights you loved strung through the treetops
taken down at the end of the holiday, intensifying your love.

# Of the Comb

It was the end of summer, the hive:
a small lighthouse,
thick with the aura of bees.
It fell with the heft of a head.
Foraged and feral, it lay open,
exposing a construction for the exquisite protection
of its queen. The boys gouged it,
tearing the immaculate joists,
dripping with the towhead honey of the acacia,
like those girls one is so fond of admiring
for having no darknesses of their own.
Do you remember that day, their laughter,
the red tiles in the courtyard at San Gimignano
like so many villages of the comb—and the girls,
lightness that offends no one
(for what is honey but the radiance of mortal things
gathered in?)—
how that morning you left, in a hurry, without stroking his
cheek,
how he left without stroking yours,
and then from across the piazza, hive-heavy with honey, you
saw him,
the piazza a welter of bee-thrum, of gold industry,
his arms outstretched as if trying to catch what was left of his
future;
and then they came,
first one, then two,
a swarm of boys descending with knives,
and the girls, morning still dangling from the hearts of their
thin leather bracelets, looked up,
the sun beating down on the dark glasses of tourists

and the glaucous leaves of the trees, and in the time it takes
honey to pour from a spoon,
his body arced up, and blood, the darkest honey of all,
spilled all his hosannas
as in coitus, when the body blazons with blood
and ready to pillage its sweetness
arcs upward, into it,
stunned.

## Space Age

My father,
his life held to Earth by thin umbilicals,
waves from his oxygen tent, his white space suit,
as monitors track the death-defying swan-dives of his blood,
calculate his odds of reentry.

Schooled in the human physics of roll and yaw,
I remembered it then,
the day my father came to explain starflight,
the auditorium curtains made of the same heavy velvet
as Scarlett's at Tara.
Paper models of airplanes reeled in air currents
like pterodactyls or mobiles by Calder.
Astronauts held by thin tethers floated in space
above ice-blue mountains eroded thin as wafers.
Houseled on stories of astrophysics and starflight—
Tiros, Nimbus—names of satellites in geosynchronous orbit,
the orchestra set sail to Mozart's tribute,
the pock-marked face of the lone band teacher rising above us
as we tongued our bright payload toward heaven.

There was never this question of reaching it then:
The moon, still uncaptured, rose
in its nightly appearance
over the manicured lawns of suburbia,
beckoned each night to its moon-girl.
No one talked of the war then.
No talk of misplaced O-rings or rocket failure,
life lessons in stability and control,
the heat of reentry. That would come later—
the future then only a question of striving.

My father,
a speck now in the mind's eye,
waves from his spit of starlight,
points to my life's center, its gravity,
the balloons of my wishes for flight held to Earth
by unforeseeable forces,
and says, *Lise, go ahead, be grandiose in life.*
*You're lovable even when no one else loves you.*
The pock-faced moon of the band teacher rises above us,
as we make our double helix back to the classroom.
We lift bright bones from our coffins to make music,
play to the laggard tempo of uneasy transcendence:
Apollo, Telstar,
the screen of the one black-and-white television silvering
as the rocket lumbers at liftoff;
and we count backwards,
*10, 9, 8, 7,*
toward a future we cannot know.

# IV

## Swimming with Eels

All summer, I watched them
make their ghostly caduceus through water—

fleeting, heraldic—
on their way to their own kingdom.

Seeing them rise out of clouds of decay,
from the lake's silk bottom

gold with an afterlife lit from within,
I thought: Even the dead lift their heads to collect sun.

Even the body carries its lantern of distances.
All my life, I have gone through this world,

a solitaria
waiting to be shown a wet road

galvanized by the body's own lightning,
clairvoyant as stone.

What flayed thing stared at me
from its button of blood,

its lidless socket,
greaved in its chain mail of lead?

I don't know what I expected to happen.
Perhaps for some god, the color of nothing,

to come rest its head on my thigh.
Long before this, I'd made my covenant.

To be left with their glistening,
I would learn to live within their circle of dread.

## Whorl and Magnet

Last night, once again, I dreamt of the white city.
In it, we stepped from the clothes of the long martyred.
We donned garments of a glistening fiber, our own nakedness,
never again to be forsaken or rent.
The trees' candelabra slowly caught fire.
Wrung until deposed from our Calvaries,
our bodies moved together in squall—
architects of moisture, the silvered flight of your hands
across breasts, our ambition for rain.
High overhead, the clocks and their surgeries
cut us with the acid bite of their chime.
I blanched. You fled. Why did we listen?
Ever since Adam, ours has been a race sentenced
to drink a draft to be made much of and let go.
Our glasses shone with the spectral aspect of the body
in X rays, the spirit's flurry housed in its *nicho* of bone.
We drank from the air in dungeons
until one gilt seed remained of magnet and whorl.

## Lakeland Blue

You have fallen in love with the smallest boy
in the class again, his eyes of lakeland blue,

and fondle him like a cool agate egg in the violet hour before
    dawn:
because you love that darkest, muskiest chamber,

its one small light at the top of the stairs
where desire, most undesired, lives—

the feel in the hand of the heart's hasp
as it fits over the U-shaped you,

the swirl of his tongue, unbuttoning each sadness inside you
as you fix your gaze at the top of the stairs.

You whom they call rubrum lily—upright, tall—
carry your burden like a mineral lode,

follow the dank odor of seaports down to the quays
where women read in your cheekbones' starveling flames

a hunger quarrying an underground river
through even the most hard-bitten ground:

because you love this boy of summer solstice and breezeways,
his voice coming across water, taking you under—

a voice of buried springs,
the short-lived evanescence of foam.

# These Windows

All your life you've been working these towns,
their houses like shards of bone,
their windows ready to flex their white sheaths
in the last hour of sundown—
these lake houses shining like glass craniums,

transfixed by a steady blue,
lapping and lapping away at the inner dark
to a calm so worn—
light tapping its scherzo, light tapping its sparkling keys
around the water's blue ground,

around the invisible chords
of these windows which say:
If you can bear your hour of openness,
you will become as pellucid as glass.
Beyond these windows' watery frames,

the cormorants pierce the shimmering,
diving as you have so long into grief,
to seize the fish which lurks like a little host
in the shallows.
And you who are carried and washed

like a diamond sutured to the dust,
move like these lake birds
who pull their wings hard
against the backs of their bodies,
slipping into and out of the lake's corrugation

until all your life's hunger, coming in almost swiftly,
makes you brindle in your sheaths,
your white facets,
like these houses
of light.

## Dona de Casa

The forest in the distance
is gently alive with their breathing,
the powdery monarchs.

I am sick, Carlos.
I wish I could say
this malaise were only cancer—
the spine stripped to the core like a palm tree
and eaten.

Lung, breath, rot of lily
beg for love, but nothing can save a fool.
In the Avenida Atlantica,
whores bloom in doorways, their magenta petals aspread
like camellias suckling bees
while the world proclaims:
belts–trusses–electric socks.

I lie here in the dark, trying to remember
what my life has brought me.
I hold myself like a dark lantern,
hoping for the life inside, the light of evening—
like the girl you first met, holding up love in my heart
like a jar of fireflies to the night.

I try to remember my loves
who no longer move me.
*Speak, speak, speak.*
I will die in my communion dress,
contracting around no one.

In September, the monarchs flock to die in these groves
like birds coming to nest.
Blinded to sing the more sweetly,
I quiver and flutter when a man puts me to his breast,
fall silent with the cloth sleep.

## Ode to a Pair of White Gloves

The hands suspect espionage, white
magic, the flavoring of vodkas with

lemon peel, dried mushroom, buffalo
grass. As if from the next room, he hears

the inaudible tinkling of crystal glass
rising: poised in moonlight,

two dead swans' heads,
albinos

pressed in an attitude of prayer.
In glove light, he rises,

passing over trees, shrubs, the oblivion
of his sleeping wife. At one end of the street,

he finds Memory waiting to receive him
like a ship.

Now they move through the streets
with the unremote gladness of hands.

The orchestra sets sail
to "Postcard from Heaven for from Two to Twenty Harps."

(Who would have thought one could find
so many harps this time of night?)

The stationary points grow dimmer.
He feels the widening of water

lap underneath him
as everyone smiles

with the conspiratorial reserve
of gloves.

# Iemanjá

Down through a night
of such sinking and testing,
down through the stick skirt
of adobe and wood houses,
Iemanjá gleams
like an abortionist's table—
teeth, milky and regular,
like the mouth of the moon.
Dona Gonsala, married to Christ,
blue at the clavicle
and blue at the wrist,
burns incense to Corcovado, the statue of Christ—
a white alpine above the jungle, an airplane of progress.
And of those awake at this hour,
a few come to greet you,
the children with eyes like cold cups of coffee
and you avoid them lest they urge the simpler solution,
lest you become like the wilder one
and drown your anxieties.
Iemanjá says, come to her waters, come to her thighs.
There are the dead ones who move
like the spirit of grace—
Maria who died from the pharmacist's work,
Paolo whose success came to him late—
all come to perform their ablutions of history.
From her position of honor in the nave of the church,
festooned with the facsimiles of various parts,
Our Lady of Sorrows looks passively on
the high priestess
who dances around an altar of sand.
Come down to her waters, come down to her thighs.
When you enter Iemanjá, don't make an effort to swim.

# How to Write a Novel

AFTER JULIO CORTÁZAR

One night, Don Geraldo dreamed a paragraph of the greatest book ever written, only to realize, that the dream being his, he must have written the text. Once, he dreamed a poem with peaks as white as the Andes, another night a list of beautiful words —deposited like sleep's alluvium but disintegrating upon waking like rotten gauze in light. Like most men, Don Geraldo might have been a great man had he only remained asleep.

About the time of these visitations, for that is what Don Geraldo called them, there was an outbreak of burglaries, small but notable for their novelty. His housekeeper remarked on the disappearance of a pomegranate she kept for the preparation of flautas, an incident not worth recounting except to mention that the housekeeper found it later, half-eaten, under her bed. Don Geraldo himself suffered the theft of the family photographs and, as he was losing his memory, the erasure of great spans of his life, leaving him with only a picture of his daughter, taken as she walked the perimeter of her walled garden, a specter of sunlight drifting across what was once her young and beautiful face. His daughter, a spinster, had refused the proposal of the town's only bachelor, the butcher. Since her refusal, it was rumored that she had been seen copulating in the Praça Nossa Señora de Paz where the dead come to kiss. The man, however, was never identified. Determined to apprehend the thieves—as if, in the act, his memory might be restored to him like some material possession—Geraldo ventured out into the garden after being awakened one night by a noise. There at the end of a stone pathway, he saw a brace of white hounds and beside them, the naked flank of his daughter moving in tandem with the elegant haunch of a hound. Startled, the daughter took out a nacre-handled knife, and with it, carved out a hunk of her breast. One of the dogs, its eyes the color of dark wainscoting, took its mistress's flesh between its jaws and, without piercing, licked the morsel clean of blood.

From here on, it should be noted, the burglaries as well as Don Geraldo's dreams of great literature stopped. He spent years trying to reconstruct them, declaring to the townspeople that inside him lay a treasure as great as that of the Sierra Madre, if only he knew how to mine it.

# The White Tiger of Vladivostok

The year snow drove a white
tiger into the city of Vladivostok
it was a month after Butter Week.

Votives guttered in their red cups,
and the body of Christ,
having exhausted its stores,

contemplated God in a transfiguring cloud.
Above earth, above ash,
the year stalled.

The tiger moved on.
It knew no Lent but hunger,
making its way through the streets

with a fastidious calm—
its fur striped with silver,
its gaze of absolutes,

all prism and thaw.
The maggot, eating only dead matter,
left in the wound only what was useful and clean.

And the soul, wearing its hairsuit of winter,
set out for the dark tundra
to be slain as poppy-red kill

by a beast born of snow.
And what penitent, self-gnawed,
would not lay down all that is dead

his prison of want,
for a glimpse of heaven's circuitry?
The tiger, having eaten,

lifted its head—
acolyte of this earth, of this dazzling air.
and as if to say: This is my gift—

so that the onlooker must look
and the seer must see—
revealed a lap of brilliance

as white as this world's flame,
a street of diamond absolutes,
concussive with thaw.

# Notes

catherinette: a woman, twenty-five years of age or older, still unmarried by the Feast of St. Catherine.

Matthew 25:1–13 recounts the parable of the five foolish and the five sensible virgins. The foolish ones, in taking their lanterns to meet the bridegroom, bring no oil, but the sensible ones take oil to replenish their stores. When their lamps go out, the foolish virgins must go back to town and are away when the bridegroom arrives.

"first chill, then stupor" is from Emily Dickinson's poem #341.

"Gary Gilmore's final words, before the life was shot out of him, were these: 'There will always be a father'" (*Shot in the Heart,* Mikal Gilmore).

*nicho:* a recess in a wall, made especially to display a religious statue or ornament; a niche.

Iemanjá: the goddess of the sea in the Afro-Brazilian religion of Umbanda.

"diamond absolutes" is from Seamus Heaney's poem "Exposure."

# Acknowledgments

Grateful acknowledgment is made to the editors of the following journals in which these poems first appeared, often in provisional versions.

*American Literary Review:* "Where Earth, This Fire," originally published under the title "Waiting for the Paraclete"

*The Antioch Review:* "The After-Season"

*Columbia: A Magazine of Poetry and Prose:* "Dona de Casa"

*The Madison Review:* "These Windows" and "Rescuers"

*The Paris Review:* "After Twenty Years of Marriage," "Conversion," "1933," "Convergence," "Labyrinth," "Swimming with Eels," and "Antediluvian"

*Passages North:* "Ode to a Pair of White Gloves" and "Iemanjá"

*Phoebe: A Journal of Literary Arts:* "Lakeland Blue"

*Ploughshares:* "Something Close"

*Sonora Review:* "Thanatos" and "Space Age"

*The Sow's Ear Poetry Review:* "Numen"

*University of Arizona Poetry Center Newsletter:* "Of the Comb"

*Western Humanities Review:* "Lingerie," "Threnody," and "Water-Hanger," originally published under the title "White Nights"

*Veer:* "How to Write a Novel"


I am greatly indebted to The San Francisco Foundation; the University of Arizona Poetry Center; the Creative Writing Institute at the University of Wisconsin, Madison, under the direction of Ronald Wallace; the California Arts Council; the Helene Wurlitzer Foundation, and The Milton Center for their gifts of refuge and support. My thanks to Joe Ahearn, Dale Gregory Anderson, Nola Perez, Donna Stonecipher and Mark Wunderlich, whose abiding faith and encouragement have buoyed me up through many a circumstance and seen me through to this project's end. To Richard Overstreet, who has served as muse for many of these poems, my thanks for his permission to use Leonor Fini's "Vision Rouge." To Carolyn Forché and Richard Howard, my utmost gratitude for their stewardship and careful readings of these poems.